I0210972

OVUM

poems by

Christine Kalafus

Finishing Line Press
Georgetown, Kentucky

OVUM

Copyright © 2026 by Christine Kalafus
ISBN 979-8-89990-308-3 First Edition
All rights reserved under International and Pan-American Copyright Conventions.
No part of this book may be reproduced in any manner whatsoever without written
permission from the publisher, except in the case of brief quotations embodied in
critical articles and reviews.

ACKNOWLEDGMENTS

"Horses," selected by Mark Doty as the winner
of the Knightville Poetry Contest, appeared in *The New Guard*
and was nominated for a Pushcart Prize.
A reprinting of "Horses" was published in 2023 by *Short Reads*
"Look Inside a Woman for the World"
appeared in the 2021 *Connecticut Literary Anthology*
"Pigtown" was published in *The Bluebird Review*

Publisher: Leah Huete de Maines
Editor: Christen Kincaid
Cover Art: Christine Kalafus
Author Photo: Christine Kalafus
Cover Design: Elizabeth Maines McCleavy

Order online: www.finishinglinepress.com
also available on amazon.com

Author inquiries and mail orders:
Finishing Line Press
PO Box 1626
Georgetown, Kentucky 40324
USA

Contents

When you start with a portrait
and search for a pure form, clear volume,
through successive eliminations,
you arrive inevitably at the egg.

Likewise, starting with the egg
and following the same process in reverse,
one finishes with the portrait.

—*Pablo Picasso*

MOCKINGBIRD

What I'm looking for is off I-95 in New Jersey
nestled between Grandpa Joe and Grandma Eva
in an all-night diner

Circling my right ring finger is a band of fake gold filigree

     Crowing will get a girl teased

Sliding the ring up past my knuckle and down again
my mother frowns across the table

     Stop that, or you'll lose it

A four-year old's idea of safety is slipping what's precious
beneath the hot rim of her plate

     We left Connecticut late

Bellies full, back on the road to Baltimore—

     My ring

Grandpa Joe swings the car around

Blue eyes bright and darting, he flies through the diner's door
wearing his bakery whites

Returning, he drapes his muscled forearms on the car's hood,
shakes his head, and twitters

     Our headlights make a V in the dark

It's cold but Grandpa Joe drives with all the windows down—
we're headed south after all

     and his cigarette is warm

He cradles my small head against his shoulder, it's solid, sculpted dough

Flicking ash to dawn, his operatic throat opens—

Hush, darlin, Grandpa's gonna buy you a diamond

A year and a half later, Grandpa Joe was under a slab outside Boston at Newton Cemetery & Arboretum

Today, when orioles build a nest on my front door, I finger my hair, tuck it behind my ear—exit elsewhere—

squint at anything that glints

CANDY LAND

Grandpa Charlie
isn't all
quarters behind the ear
piggyback rides to bed

not just a grandfather
who smiles
scrapes sugar crumb topping
off his slice of coffee cake

He lives in the Molasses Swamp

Take the Rainbow Trail over
the bedroom where my young
father protects his younger sister

Skirt the locked door to an inner room
in the basement of childhood
where stacks of Playboys mushroom

Slip through the Cherry Pitfall   there

there

Grandpa Charlie holds the deck
It's my turn
                    Choose a card

Mine is a narrow escape

SAYING GRACE

My Hungarian grandmother Rose taped school portraits
of me and my cousins on her refrigerator, row after row,
a yearbook that had its final edition when I was ten.

After her death, Grandpa Charlie kept her record—
the thin strips of cellophane tape that held us all together
browning at their jagged edges like rotten baby teeth.

After Grandma Rose's funeral, Grandpa Charlie dated Jane.
The two women had been best friends.

At holiday dinners when Grandpa Charlie vomited racist tropes
all Jane could do—he always rested his mechanic's hands on either
side of his plate—was tap him with her librarian's finger.

"He's all wrong, you know," my mother said after every holiday,
leaning down, tucking me in, kissing me goodnight on the mouth,
zinfandel mixing with the toothpaste I hadn't wiped from my lips.

After his death, I threw Grandpa Charlie's picture away, snapped
on their wedding day—Grandma Rose nowhere to be found, just
him—smiling alone in his tuxedo as if he were marrying himself.

But I kept the Polaroid of Grandpa Charlie and me together.

In it, we sit at my mother's kitchen table. I'm holding up
the construction paper family chain that Grandpa Charlie cut
before my astonished five-year-old eyes using the heavy scissors
from my mother's junk drawer.

MEDUSA, MISPLACED

I'm devouring a Pop-Tart in the living room
when my mother shrieks my name

Running into the kitchen, cinnamon in my mouth,
our eyes lock   *call the police*

My father squeezes her sprained arm through its soft cast
My mother slides down the wall

My eleven-year-old tongue turned to stone

UNBRIDLED

Flying over the Mason-Dixon Line
in my mother's Plymouth Valiant
my north takes a detour

We leave it grazing off Interstate 95

My south begins with Latin
from an over-saddled professor who fires
Agricola
Agricolae
Agricolam

Madame advances French from her barre
Grande Jété
My legs split mid-air, head back, smile high
Plié, Relevé

down
up
as if I am cantering on a horse
like the girls who wear pearls
while they muck out the stalls
the closest I will come to them

I fail on pie

It's *pah-kahn,* not *pee can*

It's expected that I covet magazines
exploding with milky dresses
echo a perfect man

Our Virginia neighbor is a survivalist
her garden an acre wide
Beside the Beltway she feeds me
rebellion

and carrots

THE CHURCH OF CHOCOLATE

"Dear God, send me some Peanut M & Ms," my mother says.

Slipping along the Blue Ridge Parkway at four thousand feet,
she grips the steering wheel at twelve o'clock.

It's Easter and we're barefoot.

A long view from a high mountain and a chocolate toast to the
future will prove the move south wasn't all for nothing.

Like gorging candy covered nuts can resurrect bouncing checks,
re-glue a broke family, fill an empty gas tank, and stop a downpour
when the forecast was sun.

Between the slashing windshield wipers, I point to the 7-Eleven.
I'm a virginal savior.

The Father and The Son glow above the linoleum: Peanut M & Ms
and Nutter Butters. Even my mother's cookies are peanut shaped.

At home, my father won't be there. At school I'll still be dateless
and our house two giant steps backward.

My breasts will ramp up their hostile takeover and my hair will
continue to resemble extra-long pubes.

Saturday nights, my mother will pour herself a thimbleful of
zinfandel, fan the pile of bills along the edge of our kitchen table.

She'll pull a few as if they are tarot cards and she isn't a Sunday
school teacher but a crap fortune teller, seeing half of what they ask.

Mom sighs a smile when I hand her absolution, when I pave over
our old union with my new confederate tongue.

We unwrap toward the summit.

SALT

On stage in the Virginia amphitheater, we dozen ballerinas balance
on the left leg, bending the working leg behind us at ninety degrees,
unnaturally turned-out so that the foot is higher than the knee.

Holding my breath and a perfect *attitude derrière*, I pray to Jesus
that the weak safety pins securing my bra inside the gauzy white
bodice succeed and that the blood-soaked Always Ultra Plus with
Wings in my tights is true to the commercial.

Even when I need the most protection, I can trust it.

Adagio is a slow dance—melancholic—like a Hollywood teenage
romance where the girl dies. Our music is cello heavy, the warm
evening's moon, light. In the wings, out of earshot of Madame,
one of the senior girls grunts and says

There they are again with that fucking dirge and coughs nicotine.

Bitch.

Madame has trained us to curtsy, to shutter our eyes, to seduce
picnickers into our tulle nets. Dirge?

The only thing dying is the day.

In the front row, a well-dressed man sitting next to Anne's mother
loud whispers *such classical features*. It's obvious he means Anne.
She who had been born fully formed into a ballerina's body.

Loading into Anne's mother's van, we steam up all the windows.
Languishing in the smell of exhaust, I'm addressing a McDonald's
French fry dipped in Anne's strawberry milkshake—*I love you*—
when I hear my name.

"The man seated next to me wanted to know who you were,"
Anne's mother says from the driver's seat.

"I told him *oh that's our new girl from up north.*"

In the rear-view mirror, her heavily lashed blue eyes
slowly lick the landscape of my head.

ALPHA ROMEO

one whiff of leather

cleaner and presto

I'm sixteen again

my first date

newly licensed

to manipulate a stick shift

in D.C. traffic not just his

imagination

the well-oiled seat sighs

when his puffed lips part

over the hand-break

his tongue enters my ear

and I know

this is one maneuver

I will hate forever

GEORGIA

I'm bent over
in our garage
head in the dryer
ass in the air
when I hear my mother
from the doorway
You cannot
Will not
Wear those shorts

Getting up early
to fold towels
before school
counts for nothing

Later at the National Gallery
in front of O'Keeffe's flowers
my ancient painting teacher
grips his beret
an affectation
he picked up in
Haight-Ashbury

Oh my god
Oh my god

he covers his open mouth
with his fine hands
I cannot even look
He's overcome

But he looks
We all do

It's very hard to see
one's own vagina
now we don't have to
I call mine
Georgia

FIGURE DRAWING

Every week, I place my easel in a different place, wanting
the back of him. But it happens as usual. When the middle-aged
male model enters the circle, having shed his robe in the doorway,
he faces me.

Sitting on the stool, one foot on a rung, the other on the floor,
hands on his knees with one arm cocked—elbow high—goddamn
if he doesn't take up all the air.

If I move, my classmates will know I'm uncool. I have few choices:
focus on that fantastic hawk nose, those tremendous caterpillar
brows, or his dick resting comfortably between hairy thighs.

Usually, I draw his face.

Compressed charcoal is hefty as a railroad pin and takes easily
to a razor. Sharpened to the point of desirability,
I use it like a wand—disappearing into the paper.

Pushing the dark medium, I lift some with a gum eraser,
coaxing the charcoal to lightness. His body blends with
my fingers, my thumbs, and both wrists until finally—fixative.

Liberally applied to contain the mess.

Hawk Nose slips on his ratty robe, changing into someone else.

He walks behind every easel, assessing. At mine, he leans in
like he's an expert. Coffee and car oil wafts off him like the greasy
dude at Hull's art supply store.

I'm breathless.

NEST EGG

Outside the sun is high and ripe.

Inside our little white house on the hill,
shaded by a line of pines, the south side is cool.

My husband and our baby were playing but sleep has overrun
and they've succumbed.

They snooze on the bed I've made while I put clothes away.
His blanched undershirts. My new elastic-waist pants.

Moving balls of half-rolled socks, I unearth the demi-cup bustier
I wore under my wedding dress.

Wrapping it around my ripped t-shirt—the one I swore I'd toss—
the only hook I can secure is at the top.

My husband's bare chest rises, his strong arms securing our baby
whose soft cheek is a built-in pillow.

I can't breathe.

WEDDING CAKE

In the death temple the surgeon skates on his diplomas

Icing my right breast, he says, *You'll be good as new*
and smacks his lips

I get a taste devouring *Keep Your Marriage Together*
and bottle-feeding our newborn twins and not brushing
our four-year old's teeth

when the scars knife to life

A forkful of fairy tale is buttery, spongy, if you don't watch it

too late   It slipped inside

swarming the bride
capturing her cathedral-length illusion veil—taffeta flash—
before lashing the buckles on the groom's shoes

and baking them in cement

Fairy tale gets everyone to sing
One! Two! She's free of all cancers and radiation tattoos!

Those unnatural freckles made by a prick
of a pin through a dollop of India ink

All her necklines plunge

PIGTOWN

Edgar Allan Poe's house stands in Baltimore
although my family's brothel was razed.
Likewise, Cousin Charlotte's speakeasy.

Pay a quarter to see a blind pig get a shot of whisky for free.
A bootlegger's ruse to avoid jail.

On a table-sized map in the city's archives,
a Maryland historian points his manicured finger,
indicating to my mother and me
where our family's buildings used to be.

She grabs my hand.
The family slum has become a football stadium.

The Ravens play a mile from the poet's grave.

Mascots Edgar, Allan, and Poe raise the crowds,
but it's his headstone bought with schoolchildren's pennies
that catches sun.

CLOCKED

at ten my mother taught me
to scrub our bathroom properly
while she worked under the table
for the wealthy
her elegant neck ticked around toilets
for cash

By eleven, I'd bolted to Saturday ballet,
flexed my body
upward in rhythms that bore
no resemblance to wiping down

Half past sixteen, I fell into a fight
between my parents in the kitchen
my mother wielding a spatula
spraying scrambled eggs on the cracked linoleum

She will go to college for whatever she wants and that's that

Up two college degrees and I still scour
from top to bottom

have I scrubbed enough
                                        that's that
but how clean is clean

WASP

A time that has never appeared on a clock is later.

There, my mother's English inheritance,
a ninety-piece set of bone china (too crazed to use),
waits for Boston Common to transform into a garden party
in honor of any man who celebrates his wife's menopause.

Later, a sting held in the gut where the Mayflower rocks
its colonial greed, keeping company with clipped articles
on Bitcoin and non-fungible tokens—undigested.

Later, a sensation akin to waving my hand over a cupcake
revering a crave, which is my generation's version of dieting.
My mother's was advised to flush dessert down the toilet.

As if drowning a desire could stop it.
As if our inheritance were only objects.
As if disregard equaled something thin.
As if pushing a lever should save us.

PAPERWORK

1. Medical exam

Q: How many pregnancies have you had?
A: *Three.*
Q: How many live births?
A: *Three.*

I write on the line designed for my signature

One miscarriage, one single child, then twins and breast cancer and chemo, you know, together, like quadruplets. But just before that—his infidelity—now our house is constantly flooding. Do you know a plumber? When I look in the mirror I don't recognize myself. Is that normal? I'm not a candidate for antidepressants. When I was prescribed prednisone for poison ivy I hallucinated.

NOTICE: YOUR DEDUCTIBLE HASN'T BEEN REACHED.
PAYMENT IN FULL IS REQUIRED BEFORE MAKING
ANOTHER APPOINTMENT WITH YOUR PROVIDER

2. Financial Exam

Congratulations!
You are approved for a mortgage from hell.

The mortgage broker smiled. Were those gold teeth?

Sign here

TILT-A-WHIRL
After Rae Rose

Aunt Gladys is an asshole. Always sure of what's proper despite
not having screaming infant twins at home and a four-year-old
who has too easily become accustomed to my bald head.
She *tsk tsks* when, every three weeks, he peels off the bandage
covering a cotton ball on the inside of my elbow.

Aunt Gladys wears a corset on her flat chest and industrial strength
garters on her skinny legs. Aunt Gladys is also imaginary.
Although not an illusion. There is a difference.

I am exiting the grocery store in February when Aunt Gladys
appears beside my cart. She doesn't help me push it into the wind.
Should have parked closer, dear. Should have worn a hat, dear.

Fuck off, Gladys, I say to the thick air. To the old man watching
me struggle I say nothing. He returned his cart and holds his car
keys. Gladys' husband, no doubt.

Once, I too, returned carts to the kiosk. My own and abandoned
ones mimicking the rusting Calder-like mobiles announcing that
this art installation plaza is from the 1970s. I'm a good citizen when
I'm healthy. When the Red Devil of chemotherapy—Adriamycin
and Cytoxan—isn't piloting through my veins.

Gladys' husband has one hand on his door handle. I stalk him with
my Mother's Eye. It has a new function as a heat seeking missile
desiring care.

I sway in the wind, loading the groceries I can't afford into the trunk.
He waits. I shove the empty cart away from me, laughing as it spins.

He shakes his car keys, "It's people like you!"

Yes. It's people like me.

HEKATE, THAT GREEK GODDESS

of antiquity beckons from inside Stop & Shop's freezer section.

What the fresh hell are you doing Hekate says.

I alone watch Hekate press her profiles—
maiden, mother, and crone—against the glass.

*We see you numbing your brain cells—one, by one, by one—with
social media. And your husband! A man who would rather
his children teethe on coffee cups than make breakfast.*

All I wanted was to buy the frozen Newman's pizza on sale.

*That because he's never there, you sometimes play with the screws
that bolt each layer of the oven door. After feeding your doughy
boys into muscled men, you nail your own meal on an Instagram
post, burning for likes at the crossroads.*

I'm backing away—every freezer door swings open.

"Leggo my Eggo," dances the waffle.
"There has got to be room in this country for a good quality
sausage," sings Jimmy Dean.

*Influencing—the new prostitution—fucking yourself over
for an egg timer from Williams Sonoma.*

BLUNT OBJECT

Let go of my wrist Oh my God get your tongue out
from between my fingers Here's some crystal—
when you cried about being divorced about missing
your kids that wasn't an invitation on my face it was pity
You ass don't say *you're so hot* my husband asleep
sweetly in front of the fire while I rinse wine glasses How
dare you pet my dog on your way to the bathroom tripping
pissing with the door open—I confess, I take pleasure in
watching your once handsome face pale when I say *I'm not
drunk not even buzzed* Do you think you could move any
slower retrieving your overnight bag your checked dress
shirt on a hanger I feel no guilt alcoholics can drive home
like they're sober But after you leave I stand on the stairs
fingernails carving moon slivers into the banister my stupid
heart unable to beat out the fear which makes me even
angrier Fuck you very much I'm female so now I'm
complicit I'm up half the night before deciding to tell my
husband—your brother—kiss that relationship goodbye
I'd ring up your ex-wife but what's the point she's gutted

WATER CURE

I

After yoga, Robin approaches my mat. Says *this is you right now*
and runs in a circle as if making a suckhole in the wood floor.
Her pouf of hair jiggles like perfectly whipped egg whites.
Robin only knows me in spandex, which is enough.
Walking home, I rescue an oak leaf from a storm drain.

II

I dig out my English inheritance—a distant aunt's collection
of Victorian thread—and delicately stitch the oak leaf's rips.

The silk thread shimmers gold against the bourbon-hued leaf.

III

At the distillery, I smear pub cheese on a volume of a Great Man's
poetry because the baby-faced millennial who owns the place
doesn't believe in napkins. All the men lick their fingers.

Silently, I retitle the Great-Man's book *Fromagerie*.
A bubble escapes my lips.

But the distiller grabs the room's attention, holding court, stroking
the throat of a newly uncorked bottle of shitake mushroom vodka
like it's a woman.

ÜKANYA

After my wedding, my father gifts me a creased sepia photo.

"This is my grandmother," he says, pointing to a sad-faced woman
sitting in a chair. She wears a white high-necked blouse.
In her arms is a blurry infant. Born in Hungary, the baby will grow
in America trading *Rózsa* for *Rose*.

Rose will embrace two more names. *Mother*—English, like none
of her ancestry. Her married name—*Lasse*—is German, like her
abusive, bigoted, unreported pedophile husband.

In the photo behind my father's grandmother stands an old woman.
She is deeply tanned, wrinkled, shrouded head to toe in black.

"That's her," I say, a lump in my throat.

Crying, I woke in the night. I was not yet two years old.
The old woman appeared in the far corner of my nursery, her head
and body draped in black, her wrinkled hands outstretched.

Comfort from a ghost is my first memory.

My father misunderstands, nodding and pointing to the infant.

"My mother lived in fear of being labeled *D.P.*," he says,
"a slur for *Displaced Person*. Or worse—*gypsy*." Grandma Rose died
when I was ten. But it's Ghost Grandmother I long for.

I touch the sepia photo often, willing her to manifest.
Eventually, I kneel in the woods.

"Come back, tell me about your cottage on the Tisza River where
you grew chamomile. Come back, teach me the folk remedy for
purging garbage from my DNA like racism and elitism and the
inborn desire for bone china which is made from actual bones."

Cow bones, but still.

"I'll fly to Hungary. I have a broom."

Nothing. Ghost Grandmother doesn't have a sense of humor.

"I'll buy a plane ticket—"

NO! Ghost Grandmother is inside my brain.

It's not safe. Hungary is riddled with rising fascism.

It's cool that Ghost Grandmother and I align politically.
I stand and wipe the dirt from my knees.

A dark figure in a long black skirt slides inside an oak tree.

There is no word in English that describes longing for
something you've never had.
In German the word is *fernweh.*

Far sickness.

There is no equivalent in Hungarian.

Conjuring this poem, I type
what is great-great grandmother in Hungarian into Google.

I copy and paste to save the umlaut.

The font is called *inherit.*

HORSES

Last week a reconstruction surgeon held my johnny coat open and said I was young in my body. He was looking at my left breast. He shifted his gaze to my right breast and said that the body doesn't like empty spaces. My right breast, once child-flat, then fertile-plump, then a tumor-less cave, now bears a scar resembling a single tuft in a cushion.

How easy, how reductive, to think of the body as decoration. How simple to paint a ceiling to hide a water stain or move a chair to protect the eye from electrical outlets—not so easy a scar that gallops from clavicle to nipple. When I met Katrina, where I lived then—in Virginia, it was at the end of high school. She loved to pair skull and crossbones patterned leggings with her hair, short and cropped. She was someone else on her horse—tailored.

We were eighteen when she put me on Boogs. Bareback. I'd never been on a horse before; it was as if I was on the roof of a skyscraper. One with the power to throw me. The next week that skyscraper threw Katrina. She's an inch shorter now. I wasn't there when it happened—I had just moved to Connecticut for college. I've always felt responsible for Katrina's fall—as if my leaving was the empty space that caused the compression of her spine.

Recently, I moved to a place that used to have two horses. When I came to view the house and barn there was only one. He stood in his stall beneath two-hundred-year-old beams—a male horse, with a female name: Lindsay. His shape was an unbroken line of mane and muscle— I touched him. Still, it was uncomfortable to look him in the eye. I didn't understand him—I'm not remotely horsey.

When I came home after the appointment with the surgeon, I stood barefoot on one of the mottled protruding stones in the yard—out behind the barn where the land is flat, clover and grass bordered by a haphazard stone wall—born, I imagine, from generations of farmers frustrated with a plow. There's a groove in the grass where the horse had been trained—a dirt oval slowly being reclaimed by buttercups. More mottled stones surround the paddock, protruding, lichen-covered, like the rounded backs of whales—only their smallest, most vulnerable part showing.

LOOK INSIDE A WOMAN FOR THE WORLD

When Connecticut shuts down, so does my uterus. "Ahh, you have Pandemic Period," my OBG/YN says. I think about punctuation while her hand is inside me.

Her first name ends in a soft *a* like *massage*, like *adore*—like *ally*.

My first OB-GYN had a last name that ended in a y, like a question, so he should have been able to listen. As if his name wasn't a trick, as if his name was a soothing *why*, as if his name didn't shout *he*. His misdiagnosis should have resulted in my death.

"That's not cancer, that's a clogged milk duct." As if the body could not build twins and also try to demolish the mother.

"My period took off on vacation," I tell Elena. She laughs and jokes back while her finger circles my cervix.

"Where did it go?" she asks, paying attention.

To myself, I answer, *I hid it like treasure, like gold, like toilet paper, like yeast—flour.*

But to her I say, "Down to Savannah, on the vacation my husband and I booked but had to cancel. No one told my period. She's been gone for months."

In a preteen memory of my mother, she chooses sanitary pads from a grocery store shelf. The box is illustrated with a painting of a woman wearing a baby doll dress, skipping at the edge of the ocean like no woman in history wearing a giant wad between her legs, even if it is labeled Stayfree. As if being a woman has ever been free.

At the height of the pandemic, there are plenty of tampons: super plus, super, and regular. There are no options with super plus and regular in the same box. If I was super plus for seven days, I'd be in the hospital—a word that contains spit so no wonder no one wants to be there.

I hold in my abdomen; I leave without buying. As if I am storing up the blood so I won't need a transfusion if or when the time comes.

As if I am storing up the blood to donate to my children, the state, the entire world.

At the end of June, the moment Connecticut's governor, who has a last name ending in a *t* like the tents he had set up in Hartford hospital parking lots, says, "Restrictions are being lifted, gently," I will be in the city's Elizabeth Park, in the middle of the rosebuds, bleeding right through my pants, oblivious, under the arbors, taking selfies—blooming.

Returning to my car, I will find that I am saturated to my thighs. Turning the key, the gas gauge reads hard *e* like *female*, like *scream*, like *money*. I'll wrap myself in the towel I use to protect the car's upholstery from my dog's wet body after hikes by the stream, pumping gas with my lower half covered in a print of mama and baby goldfish.

On store shelves, there is Charmin, Fleischmann's, and King Arthur, neatly restocked after the shortage. Everyone in the grocery is calm, in straight lines, properly masked, six feet apart—while my body spirals down into cramps. I will place two boxes of the dwindling supply of tampons in my cart when what I want to do is load box after box after box into my arms, catapult over the checkout, and steal out the store's sliding doors.

But that is next month.

Right now, Elena palpates, navigates. I'm leaning back like I just mowed the lawn, enjoying a nap in a hammock, but I'm busy writing inside my rawness, memorizing this moment of being heard. She's reading me like my uterus is braille. A word that focuses on feeling—a word that ends with a listening *e*, like the one at the end of her last name, like the one at the end of my first, like the one at the end of *circle*, like the one at the beginning of *earth*.

DEATHS

I

My father called his father *Charlie*. Never *Dad*.

When my father and his siblings were growing up,
Charlie crept into their beds. I know this much.

But there is more my father wants to say.

He phones me from his basement where he tinkers
with muscle car engines.

"When Charlie was dying of bone cancer
in the VA hospital," my father says, "I confronted him."

Through the phone comes the sound of a socket wrench.

"Charlie insisted that he didn't know what he'd done
was wrong—which is evidence that he did."

Molestation only has one name.

"The day Charlie died," my father says,
"I watched from a chair at the foot of his hospital bed."

I wasn't there, but I know how my father sits.
Feet squarely affixed to the floor, elbows on knees,
hands clasped. Thumbs in an X.

"I've only seen two people die: Charlie and Eva," he says.

Eva was my mother's mother.

"When Eva died, she was breathing and then she wasn't. Nothing
happened. I know you believe in a soul, but I didn't see anything."

In my old farmhouse an hour north, my feet are covered in a pile of
dirty laundry. I pour in the detergent.
Reminding him of my beagle, I say. "Dad, he was heavy."
"After the needle went in he floated in my arms." I say,
"A soul has weight."

Or maybe just a dog's.

I thought we were talking about Charlie. But we are not.

We are comparing our certainty about the soul.

"I've never told anyone what Charlie said when he died,
not even your mother," my father whispers.

"With his last breath Charlie said, 'Wrong way! Wrong way!'"

II

At my mammogram, I have a new copy of *Metamorphoses*
I'm not all dead   just part of me
My battle-scarred breast isn't so much resuscitated   as
exhumed   for pictures   which is what
my Hungarian great-grandmother   wanted
Two years after her third daughter   died
of tuberculosis she was brought up   into the air
her cracked pine casket   unnailed   camera ready
and my grandmother was never the same again
my father says
                                                  a gloss finish

SYSTEMA NATURAE

I would like to be efficient. Conserve family
like a Victorian lady.
Braid hair snips of my dead and secure them in lockets.

I was born half here.

Red-Winged blackbirds sing outside my house
even though they shouldn't be there. Planting eggs.
Their dominion is swamps.

Every spring the stream in our yard floods its banks.
I lie in bed, lazy, absent, the window above cracked open,
the long fingers of March brushing the top of my head.

My dead have been reincarnated as birds.
I don't get to choose my ghosts.

—*It's me. It's me. It's me.*

As a seamstress for the interior design industry, **Christine Kalafus'** sewing appeared in American *Vogue* and is on permanent display at The Mount, home of 19th and 20th century writer and designer Edith Wharton. Essays, poems, and flash nonfiction have appeared in Jessa Crispin's *The Culture We Deserve*, as well as *The New Guard* and *Longreads*, among others. "I've Heard You Make Cakes," recorded live at Laugh Boston, was broadcast on WNYC's The Moth Radio Hour. *FLOOD*, a memoir of cancer, colic, and water in the basement, was published by Woodhall Press in 2025. Christine lives in Pomfret, Connecticut.

www.ingramcontent.com/pod-product-compliance
Lightning Source LLC
Chambersburg PA
CBHW022044080426
42734CB00009B/1236

9798899903083